Letters
from *my* Wife

Letters *from my* Wife

KEITH L. PATTERSON

CITIOFBOOKS, INC.
3736 Eubank NE Suite A1
Albuquerque, NM 87111-3579
www.citiofbooks.com
Hotline: 1 (877) 389-2759
Fax: 1 (505) 930-7244

Ordering Information:
Quantity sales. Special discounts are available on quantity purchases by corporations, associations, and others. For details, contact the publisher at the address above.

Printed in the United States of America.

ISBN-13:	Softcover	979-8-90124-415-9
	eBook	979-8-90124-416-6
	Hardback	979-8-90124-417-3

Table Of Content

Dedication

This tale is dedicated to all those who suffer from dementia, and to their loving caregivers. My wife passed in 2025 from complications due to Alzheimer's. I cared for her for ten years as this awful disease slowly stole her from me. I tended to her needs and learned how to be the best caregiver I could be for this wonderful woman who changed my life.

Although I had many years to prepare for her death, when it came, I was devastated. I sank into depression and unbearable grief. This book is my attempt to pull myself out of the well of confusion and sorrow, and move beyond loss to a celebration of my wife's life and love… and continuing life.

For you, my Marianna.

Preface

This is a work of both fiction and non-fiction. Any resemblance to persons living or dead is entirely intentional. Every word is true, except for those that aren't…and even those convey truth. Life is complicated, as is the after-life.

The narrator is Keith Patterson, which happens to be my real name. The protagonist is Marianna DeCroes Patterson, her real name, and my real wife. Both of us are actual people and characters in this work of fiction. The story wanders at will between the real and the imaginary. The stories are true and made-up, and no distinction is made between one and the other.

Fiction and non-fiction. Which is it? It doesn't matter. Toward the end of the Harry Potter saga, Harry is in a train station speaking with his previously-deceased headmaster, Albus Dumbledore. Harry asks him if the train station is real or just something happening in his head. Dumbledore asks "Does it matter?"

What happens in our minds is every bit as real as things that exist independently outside us. They all affect what we think and feel and believe and hope for. We, and all life around us, is smoke and mirrors.

Our "real" bodies are mostly vast empty spaces between atoms just as the stars exist with unfathomable distances from one to the other. All is illusion of substance. All is space and energy and light.

Our minds contain worlds and the maker of worlds. The universes that exist within us are as real as those outside us. It has been proposed that we ourselves are imaginary beings in someone else's mind. Many scriptures state that God created everything out of nothing. By the power of God's mind and words were all things created. Energy transformed into light and matter.

Being made in the image of the Creator perhaps means that we too create worlds within our minds with imagination and will. This is a true story and it lives truly within my mind and heart. Welcome to my world.

Chapter One: *Her Final Breath*

I am Keith, husband of Marianna, author of "The Right Story at the Right Time," a book about what kind of stories children need to grow and mature at each stage of their development. She told stories and taught storytelling in the US, Europe and India. To say she was passionate about the power of story to uplift and help children on their way to adulthood would be a vast understatement. I loved her dearly and had the great joy of being her husband for 15 years until she passed away in August 2025.

I was with her when she died from complications caused by Alzheimer's. I held her hand, stroked her hair and sang to her while her breath shortened and then ceased. I whispered to her that it was OK to go, and asked her to be waiting for me on the other side. After I wept for a while, I helped prepare her to be picked up by the mortuary and stayed with her until they arrived. Sometimes life is painful and difficult. I was glad that her confusion was over and she was at rest. I would probably have drowned in my sorrow, but there were so many details that had to be handled…death certificates, changes to bank accounts, obituary to write, memorial service to plan, notifying everyone who needed to know, arranging for a reception at our home for people to gather after the service. Details were difficult, but they also pulled me out of my grief and depression.

Our time together was extraordinary. When we first got married, we laid out long-term plans for things we wanted to do "someday." Then, less than a year into our marriage, she was diagnosed with Alzheimer's. Suddenly "someday" became "today." We decided to do everything on our list, but right now while she was still mainly free of debilitating memory impairment. That journey was life-affirming and brought so much beauty and richness into our lives. Extended cruising in Mexico, journeys to England, France, Italy, and Spain. We walked the Camino, rode gondolas in Venice, visited the Louvre and other great museums of Europe, and had many adventures, including riding out two hurricanes in our sailboat and anchoring for days in deserted bays of uninhabited islands. We swam and snorkeled, fished and sun-bathed on our boat and slept on the deck under a double milky way and a sky lit horizon to horizon with countless stars.

It was a grand adventure, and she was a wonderful partner, full of stories and wisdom. But that's a topic for another book. This one is about something else; something most extraordinary and mysterious.

It started with a letter.

Chapter Two: An Unexpected Letter

Three months to the day after her passing, I received a letter. There were two odd things about it. There were neither postage stamps nor return address; and….it purported to be from my wife!

My first reaction was one of anger. Someone was obviously scamming me and playing on my deep attachment to Marianna. I was so sad and angry that someone would mess with me like that. I crumpled it up and tossed it in the recycling bin.

Later I retrieved it thinking perhaps there would be a clue to the identity of this inconsiderate prankster. So, I pulled it out of the receptacle, straightened and read it.

"My Dear Keith, I suppose you are more than a little surprised to see a letter from me given that I died. But I am not really dead, except that my body has passed. In every other way, I am still alive… and better than alive. I'm healthy, clear headed, happy, at peace and very, very busy. I remember your daily visits as well as those from my boys, my sisters, and friends. I saw you all,

3

but through a fog of dementia. I couldn't command my mouth to speak, but I did see and deeply appreciate your love and attention. Even now I can feel your hand in mine... perhaps if you close your eyes, you can remember mine in yours as well. Please let everyone know I saw them then and I see them now.

I cannot begin to explain how it is I can send you letters. I see your grief and suffering and it moves me. Then I think of what I'd like to tell you to ease your mind, and somehow that translates into a letter in your mailbox.

I so want to tell you about my life here, to reassure you and tell you to be happy for me, and not be sad and depressed. I hear your every thought and prayer. I see your every tear and hear every muffled sob. It's amazing. I always knew you loved me, but from here, I can actually SEE your love. It's a real and glowing light so bright inside of you. It is warm, and I can feel it still.

I have SO much to tell you. I will marshal my thoughts and send you a series of letters as I can so you will know without a doubt that we are still connected, that I am happy here, and looking forward to a future day when you can join me.

All my love. I will write again. Your Marianna."

Chapter Three: *Am I Crazy?*

I poured a couple fingers of Maker's Mark and sat down to go through the letter again. The amber liquid burned its way down my throat, and focused me. If this letter was a fake, it was very good. It looked like her handwriting and sounded like the way she wrote. But this was impossible, right?

I didn't tell anyone about it because I was sure they would think I was crazy. So, I kept it to myself and re-read it several times. By the sixth finger I mellowed out and decided I would just run with it. I chose to accept it and see where it led. I mean, why not?

Some believe in reincarnation, although it always strikes me as odd that no one remembers being a pig farmer… they always seem to be royalty. That was a frequent topic of conversation between us. She was in the "yes" camp, while I firmly believed we get one shot at the brass ring… one and done. For me that means everything I want to be, I must achieve it now. I cannot wait around for another couple of life-times to get there. Do I want to be more loving, more forgiving, more patient? If so, I feel compelled to work it out now… not in some future life.

Someone once asked me if this was a source of tension between us. Never. We talked a lot about it when we first met and decided that we had no interest in converting the other to our own point of view. We each held our own beliefs but did not push the other to believe like we did. It worked for us.

I wrote her a song about it.

PERHAPS

Perhaps we've lived together many lives.
Perhaps we've always been man and wife.
Perhaps in future lives we'll meet again.
Perhaps our joining was always meant.

I only know that when I first met you,
you felt like someone I always knew;
Like you had been there within my heart,
and we had only just been apart.

I cannot say if there are many lives we get to live,
or if there's one and only one life we are given.
I only know that now I have you in my arms.
I'll love you every moment as if I only have you for this hour.

And when the day comes that I pass away,
there's only one thing I hope they'll say;
One single entry in heaven's chart –
The man who loved you with all his heart.

And when the day comes that I pass away,
there's only one thing I hope they'll say;
One single entry in heaven's chart –
The man who loved you with all his heart.

Chapter Four: *A Second Letter*

"Dear Keith. I suppose you have countless questions about my life now. Let me tell you what my transition was like.

Unlike stories one hears, there was no light to walk into. I was in bed, feeling increasingly drowsy and distant. I was drifting toward unconsciousness but was aware you were there, holding my hand and singing Amazing Grace and Annie's Song to me. That soothed me and made me feel safe and loved. I was sad to be leaving you, but so very tired of living a half-life not able to participate and sitting there hour after hour, day after day in a fog I could not shake. I was exhausted from trying and failing to find words to reach out to you. All I could do was hold your hand and occasionally smile at you.

It was a deep relief when I finally let go and drifted off. It was like falling asleep in a warm bed on a rainy night. You just snuggle down and feel so safe and comfy. That's what it was like for me. I felt your hand in mine, and heard your voice singing me into the next life. I slept for some time, and when I later opened my eyes, I was surprised to find myself laying in a field of grass in warm sunlight.

I smelled it first; fresh and fecund, deeply rich, and earthy. I felt the grass beneath me and realized with a jolt that I was thinking clearly and feeling really rested. I stretched and it felt SO very good to feel my muscles moving after so many months of inactivity. I thought I would be weak and need help getting up. But no. I sat straight up, and was suddenly aware that there were many other people sitting on the grass around me. Startled, I looked around and was astounded to see familiar faces. Everyone I loved who had gone before me, was lounging there in the grass with me, chatting and smiling as I roused myself.

I immediately saw my mom and dad. I cannot express to you how joyful that moment was. I ran to them and wept for joy as we embraced and cried on each other's shoulders. I saw aunts and uncles, childhood friends who had died, and so many others. I did not know that I knew so many people.

In truth, many there knew me but I didn't know them at the time. Grandparents and great grandparents and so many ancestors who knew me. I came to know them over time as I met and chatted with them. They knew everything about me, of course. From heaven, we can see our loved ones and watch them celebrate and struggle. We feel their fears and love, their faith and doubts. We cheer them on and intercede to support them along their journeys.

My dearest Keith. I see you right now struggling with depression. Please, please don't be sad any longer. I am SO happy here and I want you to be likewise. I watch my sons and grandchildren as they go about their days. I smile with love and pride in them all. They think I am gone, but I'm not. I am with them, in them, around them. It's so hard to describe, but I am intimately a part of the entire world now. In some mysterious way, I am the air they breathe and the earth that sustains them. I am the rain and the sunshine. I am present in the love they feel for each other.

So hard to find the words. God is love, and I live within that love here in heaven. And since God is in them as well, I am part of their lives and bodies and relationships and feelings all the time. I am there with them and they are here in me. I love you and will write again to tell you more about my life here. I remain your Marianna."

Chapter Five: *A Mystery*

I felt so emotional as I read those words from my wife. In this life, we were a part of each other in a most tangible way. Our touches and kisses sustained us. We would smile at each other and be filled with warmth and comfort. When we kissed or made love, we left parts of ourselves inside each other. Our DNA mingled along with all the tiny entities that constitute our individual micro-biomes. We build new biomes with contributions from one to the other.

I used to smile mischievously at her and say something outrageous like "Wanna swap spit?" She'd say "Don't be so gross!" and punch me on the arm; but then she'd smile and laugh and proceed to snuggle into my arms where we would caress and kiss. We'd indeed swap spit (and other bodily fluids), laughing and smiling the entire time.

In so many ways, we were not just together, but inside each other. Our love joined us, and in a warm embrace, I could feel her body heat transfer to me as mine flowed to her. We could feel each other's heartbeats as we hugged and snuggled. I could feel her love radiating into me, and she could feel mine penetrating her heart and body and being. Our breathing and heartbeats would often synch up after a while. We were "one" with each other in so many ways.

Why would the after-life be any different? Even if I do not look up and see the sun, I know it's shining because I can feel it on my back and face. Light surrounds me, and warmth permeates my body. I can't see the photons, but I gain such a sense of well-being from them. Like John Denver sang:

> Sunshine on my shoulders makes me happy.
> Sunshine in my eyes can make me cry.
> Sunshine on the water looks so lovely.
> Sunshine almost always makes me high.

Just so, love continues after death. Marianna is with God, and God is throughout the universe and permeates everything. Thus, she is all around me too and part of the fabric of my world. I breathe her and am filled with her love even though I cannot see her any more. Still, I see through the eyes of faith.

Why not believe she is indeed watching over me and cheering me on? Why not believe she still loves me as I love her? And so, I took her letters in stride. I was either completely nuts, or she had truly found a way to communicate with me across the vast gulf of forever. If this was a dream, I did not want to wake up. If this was a miracle, I didn't want to jinx it by looking at it too closely. If this was a hallucination born out of my grief and depression, I did not want to be cured.

Life is a mystery. Love is a mystery. We don't need to understand or "solve" either one. We just need to accept them and learn to flow with them. I accepted them into my life when I met and married my Marianna. It was a wonder we found each other. And every day we were allowed to share with one another was a blessing and a miracle. Why not one more for the road? Who says death is an end to the story? I believe the tale continues, and she is still weaving it to lift my soul.

My love, you made my life and my story better. I look forward to hearing more tales. I will await your next letter.

Chapter Six: A Memory

During our courtship as we were getting to know one another, it quickly became clear to me that of all her skills and experiences, storytelling was the most important to her. She insisted that stories were the key to reaching children and guiding them along the path of their self-discovery of purpose in life.

I asked her for an example. After a bit of thought, she told me the following true story. A new child (we'll call him Jason) joined her class and was having a difficult time making friends or becoming part of the class. Jason often isolated himself during recess. The other children would play games, and invite him to join. But he would withdraw and sit alone on the ground near some trees and spend his time digging in the soil and looking at worms and bugs, dragonflies and butterflies.

How was she going to integrate this shy child into the class? One afternoon during their science lesson, she told the story of Luther Burbank's childhood. He was an awkward child who spent his time alone down near a lake. He would endlessly watch the insects and other critters that lived at the edge of the lake. He saw butterflies leave their eggs. He watched every day until they hatched. He saw caterpillars inch along eating leaves, then eventually attach themselves to the underside and build a cocoon from which they would eventually emerge as a beautiful butterfly. He paid attention to nature.

As she told the tale, she saw the other students look at the new boy with renewed interest. One afternoon, several students wandered over and sat with Jason in the dirt. He explained what was happening there in the soil and what the insects were doing. They found new respect for him, and he discovered he could share his interest with them. A story changed their lives.

I was impressed. As we walked along a mountain trail, I challenged her to make up a story then and there. She led me over to a stand of California Live Oaks and we sat in the shade of the largest tree on a bit of grass. This was obviously the oldest tree since it was much bigger, with branches stretching out in all directions. This is the story she made up.

> In ages past, there were no trees on this hill. Raven looked around and said "I must fly too far every day to find tasty things to eat. It would be nice to have a shady tree right here where I could harvest nuts and find juicy bugs." And so, she flew far away to where she knew there were strong and ancient oaks. Raven picked up a large acorn in her beak and flew back to this very hill where we are sitting right now. Right over there, she dug a hole, and tucked that acorn into it. Every day, she brought a beak-full of water to moisten the soil. After tending it for some time, a tiny sprout inched its way up out of the ground. Raven would check on it from time to time, and was pleased to

see it grow first into a small, supple sapling, then eventually into this strong and shady mother-tree. As it grew, it produced many acorns and soon an entire forest spread out across the hilltop and the meadow below. The oak was generous with its branches. She gave a home to many birds, squirrels, and other creatures of the forest. Eventually, people arrived and she sheltered them as well providing them with cool shade in the summer, and a canopy against the rain to weary travelers who sought her out for her welcoming wide-spread arms.

I think that was the moment I fell in love with her. She had within her multitudes and all life. These tales inhabited her soul. They awaited her to give them birth and bring them forth into the world where they could work their wonder.

Chapter Seven: *I Want to be Seen*

I asked her why she thought stories were so important for raising children. She told me it was because stories don't have to come in through the mind and logic. Stories bypass that mechanism and go straight to the heart. They live within the children even if they are unaware of it. The tales build a framework inside their minds and hearts, and provide them with a way to see reflected their own problems and doubts, and find, almost instinctively, how to navigate their way through life's challenges.

I asked her how she could know what they needed and wanted. She looked at me and smiled, and told me that all children, all people want one thing above all else: To know that they are seen…to know they are valued and loved…to know that they matter.

I was gob smacked. I thought that was a most wise and profound answer. I had deep respect for her intelligence, empathy, and creative instincts.

Once more, I responded to her with a song.

I Just Want to Be Seen

Quietly she said, "I just want to be seen;
so open up your eyes and look at me."
Quietly she fell into my waiting arms.
"I see you, love, with all my searching heart."

Ain't it funny how you find exactly what you need
When you open up your heart to the possibilities?
Ain't it wondrous how the light fills your soul from above,
When you open up your heart to love?

Make a loom of words and weave me a tale.
Explore the distant boundaries of your soul.
Bind my heart to yours with ephemeral thoughts
wrapped around my body like a robe.

Ain't it funny how you find exactly what you need
When you open up your heart to the possibilities?
Ain't it wondrous how the light fills your soul from above,
When you open up your heart to love?

Eyes of blue and gold are gazing up at me:
the richness of the earth and the deep, abiding sea.
My love, you're such a warm and wonderful surprise:
the universe unfolding in your eyes.

Ain't it funny how you find exactly what you need
When you open up your heart to the possibilities?
Ain't it wondrous how the light fills your soul from above,
When you open up your heart to love?

From the beginning, we seemed to find and feed something inside one
another.

Chapter Eight: *Judgment*

"My dearest Keith. I remember feeling apprehensive about my final judgment. I had visions of standing before God, angels and a host of others while my entire life was reviewed in public. Would I be worthy of heaven? Would I stand humiliated as everyone saw my life unfold? They would see all my sins and foibles. I would be humiliated. Had I been good enough for heaven, or would another fate await me?

I need not have worried. Evidently, my heart weighed less than a feather. Do you remember that story I told you of Anubis from Egyptian tradition? Of course you do. Well, the moment was not like that, nor did I stand before a throng of observers while my entire life was laid bare. There was just this instant where I felt God's light and presence fill me, shining into every corner of my soul. God's soft, reassuring voice thundered through me to my bones. I was shaken, frightened and reassured in the same moment.

I felt as fragile as a butterfly and as immovable and deeply rooted as an ancient tree. In a single flash, God lifted me up and embraced me as one would a small child. I felt instantly reassured, warm and safe in surrounding arms. In that instant I saw all those I had loved and cared for. I had a vision of light and energy flowing between us. We were connected by love. In that moment I saw every child and grandchild, every student and peer, even strangers to whom I had given nothing more than a smile and a friendly greeting.

It was a vast crowd and I could see every one of them, and the repercussions of those moments of connectedness. I saw how even small acts of care and kindness rang like a bell into every corner of their lives. We were, all of us, joined by love experienced as a warm, surging light that flowed back and forth between and among us all. And not only us. What was shared in those moments passed on from them to the multitude of others that inhabited their worlds. The love spread on and on to the far horizons. Every act of love and kindness multiplied and amplified through them into the lives of all who they, in turn, drew into their circles of love and trust.

I saw all this in a single instant as I melted into God's arms reassured that I had lived a life of love, and that I indeed was where I belonged. Not only my heart, but every fiber of my being felt light as a feather, and God's soft voice rumbled through me again: "Welcome home, my dear, dear child."

That was it. That was my judgment. It was never anything to fear. Rather, it was a culmination of a life of love for family, students and so many more. We were all here... both those in heaven and those still on earth, joined by a love that overcomes all time and distance.

I love you, my dear husband, even more than before. Can you feel my hand in yours? Can you sense my presence as I surround you with hugs and reach into your heart to heal and strengthen it? I know you can. So, stop grieving. You are loved. If I could, I'd slap you upside the head like Cher in Moonstruck, or Gibbs on NCIS. "What's the matter with you?! Wake up!" It's a loving smack of course, but I need to get your attention. You deserve to be happy and loved. Don't cry over my departure any more. Smile. Remember our love and adventures and know that I am watching over you.

Do not fear your own judgment. I love you deeply; and so does God and so many others here in heaven and there on earth. Keep loving and smiling and spreading joy wherever you can. Your Marianna."

Chapter Nine: *A Smile and a Piece of Trash*

I once told Marianna that in my view, there are three kinds of people in this world: those who live in the past, those who live in the present, and those who live in the future. I told her that those who live in the past are living in a dream world where everything is already "done." They can't change or manipulate it, nor can they profit from it. In my view, they were just reminiscing and indulging in daydreams.

Then there are those who live in the present. I told her that these people are short-sighted and will forever be a victim of "the way things are." They try to navigate the world around them but are stuck in a reactive mode of living.

Finally, there are those of us who live in the future. Looking ahead, planning. We have our sights set on what the future can be, and figure out how we can contribute to it and help build that future. These are the movers and shakers.

She listened, smiled, then told me the story of the three blind men who encountered an elephant. One felt the tail and said "This is a snake;" one felt the side and said "This is a wall;" and the third felt a leg and said "This is a large tree." The conclusions were reasonable given their limited input… but they were all wrong. They each only experienced one part of the elephant and failed to perceive the whole picture.

She laughed and hugged me and said "I like the way your mind works; but in this case, you couldn't be more wrong." I bristled at that, but asked her to set me straight…perhaps with an edge of sarcasm.

"Do you have a soul?" I said yes. "Do you believe in God?" Yes. "Do you believe that you live in God and God lives in you?" I do. "And will you be joined with God in heaven?" I believe that. "In that case, you are part of love and all time past and future. You live in a present, informed by your past, and planning for your future. You live in all three at once – welcome to your elephant." Then she laughed and hugged me.

She was always so good at seeing through me and guiding me away from the dead ends my false conclusions had led me. She told me to change the little things I could today to make my little corner of the world a better place.

And so I did… with baby steps. I saw a crumpled piece of paper on the ground and disposed of it in a trash can. I heard a street musician playing an accordion – Don't Worry, Be Happy. I wandered over, smiled and sang along, then dropped $20 in his tip jar. Small gestures of love. I apologized to a co-worker for belittling their ideas about how to improve a project we were working on, and asked them to have a cup of coffee with me and help me understand what they wanted to do. Small actions that let people know they are seen and valued. How'm I doing, Marianna?

Chapter Ten: *The Story that Wanted to be Told*

I once asked Marianna where all her stories came from. It seemed they were endless. In her case, she had read so many stories over the years that they embedded themselves in her and made her sensitive to tales that were brewing inside her. She immersed herself in works like Rumi's poetry, Harun and the Sea of Stories, The Power of Myth, Greek/Roman/Norse mythologies, and hundreds of other sources. She absorbed them and allowed them to take root in her mind, heart, and imagination.

She told me that stories were doorways into our own souls. They allow us to see ourselves and the world through the lens of other people and cultures. They broaden our perspectives and grant us alternative ways of looking at our own lives and problems. Often, a story can give us a new way to be in the world and tackle challenges that may seem to be insurmountable.

She said that there were far more stories floating around in her soul than she could ever have time to write down. I asked her where they come from? She told me something extraordinary. She said to think of them as if they had a life of their own. They exist "out there," and were waiting for someone to notice and give birth to them.

I asked her where I could find such stories and she said to just "pay attention." She told me to believe that they are out there and searching for someone to give them voice. I was fascinated by this concept. She said there was a story out there waiting for me to give it voice. She noted that I was a very tactile person and that if I wanted to give birth to a story, I should seek out a place that would allow me to pay attention to my senses and just ask the story to speak through me.

I thought that was a woo-woo crock, but she had shown herself to be insightful and wise. I chose to believe her and test it out. So, we drove to a redwood forest we often enjoyed walking in. We sat on the sorrel growing at the base of a tree. She had me close my eyes and pay attention to the redwood bark, the smell of the forest, and the subtle silence of the woods. She told me to start talking. This is what spilled out of me.

It's Time

The old man was thinking about his life, and felt in his bones that he had not much longer to live. His grandson loved him dearly and would often come to visit and play chess. And so, on a chilly summer day along the northern California coast, the grandson drove the old man to a favorite Redwood stand they had often hiked. When they arrived and parked deep in the forest, he asked the young man to wait in the car for him. He wanted to make the short walk to their favorite cathedral grove under his own power. The grandson was a bit apprehensive but knew there was no point in trying to dissuade him. Once his mind was made up, it was made up.

So, the old man took his cane and walked slowly up the short path to the place he had first encountered his wife so many years before. They had met there serendipitously as they both marveled at the towering trees. They smiled at each other and it was almost love at first sight. They courted, married, and raised a fine family; but she had passed away nearly a decade before. The old man missed her still but sensed he'd be joining her soon.

He sat at the base of the largest tree, closed his eyes, felt the welcoming embrace of the soft redwood bark behind his back, smelled the wonderful aroma of the sorrel, and drifted off to a restful nap in the arms of the forest he so loved.

Now, back in the parking lot, the grandson was playing games on his iPhone and noticed in the car's rear-view mirror that a beautiful young woman had wandered up to the parking lot and was sitting on a picnic bench. She was eating a snack, and he was thinking of walking over to introduce himself to her, when another young man jogged down the upper path. They waved at each other. As the happy youth passed the car, he leaned down and gave the young man a pleasant smile and a greeting. He smiled back, but was disappointed to see him jog over to the young girl and watched them embrace and share a kiss before they headed out down the lower trail. He didn't have a girlfriend yet, but hoped he'd find someone like that to share his life one day.

After some time, the grandson got restless and a little concerned that his grandfather had not returned yet. He got out of the car and walked up the path. He knew where the old man would be. That cathedral grove was part of the family lore and they'd all visited and picnicked there. Much to his surprise and consternation, the old man was not there. He saw the cane leaning against a tree, but had no idea where his grandfather was. He called out to him and walked around the area for several minutes, but found no hint of where the old man was.

He drove back to the ranger station and explained his concern that his grandfather might be lost. They immediately started a search of the area. The young man also called his family, and they all drove up to help with the search. For three days the rangers and volunteers searched high and low. They checked places he could possibly have fallen into but no sign of him was ever found.

They finally gave up and declared that he was most likely dead and that some hiker or other would eventually find his body. All kinds of theories popped up to explain his disappearance. The rangers were convinced he had gotten confused and wandered off. The Miwak natives said there were legends of redwoods that looked over the forest and would sometimes manifest themselves as a human being, living among us for many years before returning to the forest to resume their task of watching over the woods. Of course, this being California, there were no lack of theories that he had been abducted by ghosts or aliens.

As for me, I have another theory entirely. I think he returned to the place where he found his wife and his joy. He was prepared to go to sleep there and join her in heaven. And so, he did indeed fall peacefully asleep with memories of his young bride in his mind. But something most curious happened. As he sat there and breathed in the familiar scents and smiled at the visions of his wife and their life together, he suddenly realized that he was no longer struggling to breathe, and with each deep breath, he was feeling stronger.

He opened his eyes and realized he could easily stand, and that he no longer needed his cane. In fact, as he looked down at himself, he could see he was straighter and stronger than he'd been in many years. He suddenly knew what he had to do. He jogged down that path and as he came around the last bend, he could see his wife standing on the far side of the parking lot. He jogged past the car where his grandson was waiting, smiled at him, and gave him a jaunty wave before crossing the lot and embracing his dearly loved wife.

The forest had renewed him and he knew he was about to enjoy another great life with his dear, dear wife. Personally, I think that's the explanation for what happened all those many years ago. And I should know, for I am he. Now my wife and I are old once more, and we're thinking it's just about time to go for a walk in the woods.

I have no idea where this story came from. It just popped into my head like Marianna said it would. I guess it was just a story that wanted to be told.

Chapter Eleven: An Unexpected Visit

"Dear Keith. I had a most unexpected visit the other day. Your parents sought me out! Your mother, of course, knew me as I knew her from our shared time on earth. But I'd never met your father since he passed away long before we met. I must tell you: he is -so- funny. He keeps me in stitches with his string of jokes and puns. I can see his sense of humor in you. You look a lot like him.

They both gave me great big hugs and thanked me for loving you so well. I wish I had known your father while we were together. Barbara told me he used to have a pet parakeet. It liked to sit on Calvin's sparsely-haired head and talk incessantly. Evidently, your father taught him to speak. He'd sit on your dad's head and say things like "Pretty boy," and "I love you." He kept trying to teach that bird a complicated phrase, but he never quite got it right. He wanted Petey to say "Absolutely preposterous." He would say "Absolutely, absolutely, pre-pre-pre-pre" but could never get the whole word out. It was a source of great amusement to listen to him try again and again to get it... but he never did.

Your parents also told me many stories about you. Calvin said he always knew you would never be a good fisherman. He took you to the Huntington Beach Pier early one morning and got the both of you all set up for a day of fishing. After about a half hour, you looked up at your dad and asked "Dad, what time do the fish bite?" Calvin and other adults nearby were almost apoplectic with laughter at the innocence of your childish question.

[Author's Note: In my defense, I was only 7 and had read an article that said large fish chase small fish, small fish chase plankton, and plankton float helplessly with the tides. Thus, when the tides move in or out, so do the plankton. Small fish follow, and large fish come to dine. Therefore, if you know the local tides, you know when you'll be more likely to find large fish hunting for a meal. I had the right idea, but I didn't know how to explain it. So, I just shut up, smiled sheepishly and put up with the laughter. Kind of a pattern throughout my life. If my ideas were met with mockery, I'd just smile and keep to myself rather than try to defend and justify my remarks. Even if I -knew- I was right, I would rather just hold that to myself, rather than deal with conflict. My dad used to say "God gave you one mouth and two ears so you could listen more than you speak. If you shut up and listen, pretty soon you'll know twice as much as the other guy." Thus, my stock reply through the years has been "Hmmmm, perhaps you're right" even if I knew they were wrong. If I ever say to you "Interesting idea, perhaps you're right" you should know that I mean something very different. My dad's belief that I'd never become a fisherman became a self-fulfilling prophecy. I felt so humiliated being the butt of the adult's laughter that I never tried to learn how to fish again.]

Your mom told me stories too. She said that one day when you were about 10 or 11 you got a little too big for your britches and sassed her one too many times. She went out front and stripped the leaves off a small, flexible branch from the acacia tree. This was her makeshift swatter. When she called you to come in, you ran to an apple tree in your back yard and climbed way up inside it. She marched over to the tree and said "Keith Lee Patterson, you come down here right now!" (The use of my middle name was a dead giveaway that she was -really- mad at me.) You refused to come down until she told you she'd tell your father and let him deal with it if you didn't come down right now. You descended and received your swats in silence. In truth, she told me that she had a hard time not laughing at the ridiculous situation with you up the tree, and her waiting below swinging the switch back and forth.

I enjoyed our visits. I learned much about you from their stories. They were always proud of you and loved you like crazy... just like me, my dear heart. Until my next letter, I remain your Marianna."

Chapter Twelve: *Family*

I was thankful that Marianna and my folks had connected. Family is complicated. What constitutes family? You can begin with DNA. Two people mate and create a child. Family by blood. But before that, the parents met and perhaps decided to marry and have children. Family by law. What if they don't marry? Still a family by commitment and love.

What if that couple adopts a child? Family by adoption. What if one of the children's friends spends much time with the family and comes to feel like a part of the family? Life binds them all over time and they become like members of the family through the power of love.

My eldest son had a friend like that. So much so that when we were preparing to move from California to Virginia with a job transfer, the kids begged me to take him with us. I spoke with his mother, and she agreed that he could come. Thus, he became part of the family and moved with us. Family by affiliation.

I had a work colleague with whom I shared many values and goals. We've now known each other for 50 years and we tell everyone that we are identical twins which is patently absurd. There are obvious differences in height and appearance so that being identical twins seems unlikely. And yet, we are. We are identical in our hearts. There's nothing I wouldn't do for him, and he for me. We are family by attitude.

When Marianna was a teacher, she took on tutoring as a means of supplementing her salary. With one such student, she became a second mother. They spent a great deal of time together and did things bake and brew, build and learn. He was more than a student; he became a family member. Family by shared experiences.

We draw many into our inner circle throughout our lives. They become included in the family. Family by love. Family is difficult to define and limit, but one thing is certain… it includes more than just those related through blood or adoption. If we are lucky, we learn to open our hearts and our arms to others and draw them into our circle of love, as they draw us into theirs.

Maybe that's the point of life. Draw others into the protection of our inclusive love forming an ever-widening circle of friends and family. Perhaps we are all family if we only have hearts big enough and understanding deep enough to perceive it. Perhaps instead of being adrift in a sea of strangers or enemies, we are all family but have failed to perceive, acknowledge, and live it.

I do like that idea. Perhaps, dear reader, you and I are family, but we just don't see it yet.

Chapter Thirteen: A Mission

"My dear husband. Not long after I arrived here, I discovered something that led to my mission. Why, you may ask, would someone need a mission in heaven? Is not everything perfect there? The fact is, we carry with us the need to be busy with things that matter to us. I assure you, we do not sit around playing harps and singing Hallelujah. The praise that is offered to God is not all in the form of words and song. The praise is our very existence and living always in the love shared between God and ourselves.

It may surprise you as much as it did me, to find that some individuals arrive frightened and disoriented. Not long after I got here, I came upon a young child who was scared and confused. She had died at a very early age after a brief illness. She did not understand what had happened and where she was.

I did what I always do when I see a hurting child. I took her by the hand and we sat down together under a shady tree. There I held her and spoke soothingly to her. I told her stories. I told her about the lost little girl crying because she did not know how to get home; and how the forest animals took care of her and made sure she got home. I told her about Wendy and the Lost Boys of Peter Pan. We did some fun finger stories like the Itsy Bitsy Spider, and Where is Thumbkin?

That amused and calmed her. She was still sad that she could not be with her parents, but I showed her how she could see them and know how they were doing. She was sad at their sorrow, but I taught her how to hold them in her mind and heart and she could see for herself that her reaching out soothed her parents' suffering.

Much to my surprise, I saw that other residents had gathered 'round to hear the stories too. And not just them. I caught glimpses of angels hovering nearby and listening in as well. It appears that heavenly hosts enjoy a good story too. A young couple came up and offered to take care of the little girl. That's how it is here. People see a need and just step up to meet it. We are all connected and bound by love for each other and God. When there is a need for love, there's no shortage of those willing to share it.

Thus was born my mission. I wander all about Heaven always on the lookout for a lost or lonely soul. I take them under wing, and help heal and orient them with carefully chosen or crafted stories. I've heard angels and other residents refer to me as "God's little storyteller." As I was on earth, so I am in Heaven.

Now, residents, both human and angelic, search me out and bring confused or disoriented newbies to me so I can calm, orient, and ground them. Everyone has a "mission" here consistent with who they were on earth. I guess I have become the unofficial storyteller. How perfect for me.

You might imagine I would have difficulty talking with those who speak other languages. Not so. We are beings of light, energy, and love. Communicating is heart-to-heart without need for physical language. Each speaks in their familiar tongue, and everyone hears them in their own. It feels like the Gospel story of the Apostles speaking to a crowd gathered from all corners for the religious high holy days. Each one heard the message in their own language. The Spirit bypassed the need for translators. Here, love accomplishes that.

Until next time, know that you are in my heart always. Your Marianna."

Chapter Fourteen: *Food for Thought*

Marianna was correct. I had never imagined that there would be people lost and disoriented in Heaven. I figured that once they were admitted through the pearly gates, they would know everything they needed to know.

The fact that everyone keeps busy with their "missions" totally escaped my imagination. But it makes sense. I would be totally bored without something to absorb me. Give me a garden or a piece of paper so I can grow some plants or write songs. Let me have musical instruments and other voices with whom I can harmonize. Who knows, maybe I WILL be one of those sitting around playing harps and singing hymns of praise. That just might be the heaven awaiting me.

Maybe I'll have time to learn all the instruments I never got around to. I play guitar, bass, accordion, recorder, piano, organ, dulcimer, zither and autoharp. Maybe a couple others. Not great at any of them, but well enough to amuse myself and be able to uplift my wife. I'd love to learn harp, violin, and cello. Why not brass instruments while I'm at it? The French horn is awfully sexy. I wonder if "sexy" is a thing in Heaven.

Perhaps there, I can pick up more instruments and add them to my repertoire.

That's exciting to think about. Maybe I'll be able to continue learning in Heaven. How great would that be, to continue learning new things? As the famous physicist Feynman said (more or less): "Given the choice between understanding all the secrets of the universe, and searching for them, I'd choose to search." It's the thrill of discovery that's rewarding.

Now that I'm learning so many unexpected things about Heaven, I find my mind wondering. Are there pets in heaven? How about aliens? I mean, they may be out there living their lives right now. Do they have an afterlife? If so, is it in this Heaven, or are there many heavens to meet the needs of wildly differing species?

Do husbands and wives still share carnal pleasures? From what my Marianna has been telling me Heaven is still a place of sensations. She spoke of waking up on the sunlit grass, fragrant with the scent of loamy earth. She sits under a shady tree to tell stories. Do husbands and wives hold hands and make love? Since beings there are made of light and energy, perhaps there is no desire for carnal relations. So many questions her narrative is raising, but no way to send them to her.

I am so relieved to learn of her happiness in Heaven, and her discovery of a mission so she is engaged and fulfilled there. I guess I always thought of heaven as a place where we would be happy, but I never gave much thought to what form that would take. Her stories are uplifting, informative, and more than a little surprising.

And comforting. It dawns on me that I am not grieving as much as I did before her letters. Her messages reassure me she is well and happy. That takes a heavy weight off my shoulders, and brings me much joy.

Chapter Fifteen: *Aliens....in Heaven?*

My wandering mind returned to a previous thought. Are there aliens in Heaven? I know, that's a strange thought, but it somehow sticks with me. It is a semi-serious concern for theologians.

The Vatican has papers on the topic. If aliens exist, do they need salvation? Did Jesus die for their sins as well? What is the religious response to our first contact with beings from another planet. It may seem to you that I made up that last bit, but it's true. Theologians have argued weighty topics such as how many angels can dance on the head of pin (also true).

In an episode of Young Sheldon, the pastor of their Baptist church was asked, "If there are 8-legged aliens out there, did Jesus die for them too?" He had no answer right away but checked with theologians and came back with this answer. If there are 8-legged aliens perhaps they never fell out of communion with God and thus do not need salvation. But if they -do- need salvation, then the Son of God would appear to them in a form familiar to them, to save their 8-legged souls.

So I guess that more or less answers my odd question. There would be no aliens in the Heaven inhabited by my wife. If they have an afterlife, it would undoubtedly be in a heaven that would be comfortable and familiar to them. If we posit that God is infinite, then he/she/them would appear like them in order to be accessible to them. And their heaven would be a familiar place to them.

That sort of smacks of segregation to me. But what do I know? I'm just a searching writer, not an educated theologian.

But I do wonder about pets and non-human life forms on our own planet. In many cases, pets really are our fur babies. We are attached to them and they to us. That's certainly a loving relationship. And if love is there, why not imagine it continuing in Heaven?

How about apes and whales and other intelligent species on earth? Do they have souls? Do they have a heaven to go to? How about our pre-human ancestors? At what point in evolution did we evolve into a species that is heaven-bound? What flipped the switch as it were? And if there was no evolution and God just created us as we see ourselves now, are we the only beings here needing salvation?

Beings that many purport to be our human ancestors such as Denisovans, Neanderthals, Cro-Magnons and others had creative impulses. They made tools, built places to live, and made art. Do they have an eternal existence? Marianna hasn't mentioned seeing any in heaven but that doesn't mean they are not there.

I love how Douglas Adams put us all in our place when he wrote in his 5-book trilogy that started with The Hitchhiker's Guide to the Galaxy, that earth was created to host mice who were part of a vast computational network seeking the answer to life, the universe and everything. Humans were just after-thoughts on the planet really created for the mice. (By the way, if you're wondering about the answer, it's 42).

Chapter Sixteen: Canyons of Clay

"Dear Keith. You'll never guess who I spent time with today. I encountered the mystic Kabir in my wandering. You remember me talking to you about the poetry of the mystics like Rumi and Kabir, I'm sure. They really understood God in a way that is different from western visions. I know you remember Kabir's "Clay Jug" because you memorized it and even included it in a song you wrote for me.

Inside This Clay Jug by Kabir

Inside this clay jug there are canyons and pine mountains, and the maker of canyons and pine mountains!

All seven oceans are inside, and hundreds of millions of stars.

The acid that tests gold is here, and the one who judges jewels. And the music that comes from the strings that no one touches, and the source of all water.

If you want the truth, I will tell you the truth: Friend, listen: the God whom I love is inside.

I loved how you incorporated those references in the song you wrote me about walking the Camino. That journey across Spain was a search for God within in and all around me. It was a spiritual journey that I loved so much I walked it a second time with you.

You remember how hard, hard that was? The exhaustion, the blisters, the getting lost and finding our way back to the path, the people who helped us along the way. Wasn't that just a perfect experience of what our lives are about. We meet others, we meet God, we meet ourselves in our daily Camino through life.

I loved sitting with Kabir and talking about his poetry and how indelibly it was imprinted on my soul during my earthly journey. I tried to sing that song you wrote, but I'm afraid I rather butchered it. But it amused him anyway.

From heaven, I can now so clearly see the spiritual journey that our Camino was. You are still on your Camino, my dear husband, and I watch your every step. Find God in those you meet on your daily journeys, and continue to seek joy and peace and love. I can see you are still suffering grief from losing me, but please try to move beyond that, my love. I am -so- safe and happy here. Every day, every moment is a joy in God's presence. Here, I am fulfilled and surrounded by love.

You are too, but your grief is blocking your ability to see it. Please rejoice for me and lift your eyes up. Don't be downcast, hanging your head and looking at the ground in sorrow. Raise your sight to heaven, smile at the beauty all around you, see the love of those who surround you. You are loved on earth and in heaven. Please lift your mind, heart and thoughts from your troubles and find joy again in love of nature, others around you, and inside yourself.

Know that I love you and lift you up every moment of every day. Until next time, I remain Your Marianna."

Chapter Seventeen: Camino

I remember every day of our trek across Spain. It was -so- hard and yet -so- joyful. We were exhausted at the end of each day's walk when we would tend to our blisters and rest from the effort, enjoying the wonderful company of fellow Caministas. I remember being so astounded at the range of ages, the ethnic mixes, the infinite reasons why each traveler chose this demanding trek.

Truthfully? There were days we wanted to give up and go home. But we did not. We pressed on through the heat, the discomfort, the pain, the discouragement. Then we capped off our journey with a few days in Venice where we explored that city, its architecture, and food. I remember we took the obligatory gondola ride through the canals but instead of the gondolier singing to us, I stood and serenaded you with John Denver's "Annie's Song." I even got a little applause from some folks walking along beside the canal. But Marianna's smile and the love in her eyes was all the appreciation I needed.

Camino

I am on a Camino; I am seeking a way
through mountains and forests, and canyons of clay.
O'er mountains and rivers of deep greens and blues;
I travel Camino alone and with you.

> We are all on Camino from the day of our birth.
> We seek ourselves and each other, we want to learn our true worth.
> We are all on Camino, every day of our lives;
> Whether we are all strangers, or close as husbands and wives.

I am on a Camino, I am seeking a truth
I have hungered and yearned for from the days of my youth.
I am on a Camino, I have traveled alone.
Take my hand and walk with me, as we two journey home.

> *(…with apologies for my butchered Spanish…)*
> Todos vamos camino de dia naciamento,
> nos encontrarse y otros; sabemos valia nuestro.
> Todos vamos camino cada dia de vida;
> como todos foresteros o esposos y esposas.

Our search for each other is a search for ourselves.
We complete one another; we're each other's true wealth.
Like flint and like fire, like morning and night,
we each need the other to balance our lives.

> We are all on Camino from the day of our birth.
> We seek ourselves and each other, we want to learn our true worth.
> We are all on Camino, every day of our lives;
> Whether we are all strangers, or close as husbands and wives.

I wrote that for Marianna regarding my thoughts about Kabir's poem, and our Camino across Spain. Lord, I loved writing songs for my wife. She told me the most wonderful stories, and I created songs I sang just for her. They probably weren't very good, but they were a secret love language between us. That imbued them with meaning and beauty for the both of us.

I love that old saw: Sing like no one is listening, dance like no one is watching. We privately danced and sang our way through our marriage. We weren't performing; we were making love. Walking, holding hands, telling stories, singing songs. These creative activities were part of our journey.

God, how I miss her hand in mine, her smile, and her kisses. She writes me comforting messages and tells me not to grieve, but how can I not have a huge hole in my empty heart without her in my arms? Can anyone out there tell me that?

Chapter Eighteen: In the Beginning

I'm reminiscing, looking at photos of Marianna across the years, bathing in the simple pleasure of looking at her images and recalling our joy. We did so many simple things during our courtship.

We drove to nearby hiking trails to enjoy nature and walk hand in hand, talking about what was important to us. The dance of discovery; smiling at one another as we explored common ground. She picked up an acorn and spoke of the miracle of life. It contained all the instructions it would need to become a strong oak. We identified wild flowers, enjoyed the variety of shapes and colors, and admired the way butterflies hovered about, and watched a hummingbird systematically visit every flower on a plant.

We were childlike, laying on our backs in a grassy field and staring up at a perfect blue sky with clouds drifting by. We exercised our imaginations, telling each other what the cloud shapes brought to mind.,

Our most memorable outing was a train trip from Emeryville to Sacramento and back. It was a spur of the moment thing. We were out driving around, and she mentioned to that she loved trains. I said "Well, let's go for a train ride right now." She laughed: "Are you kidding"?

Nope. We drove to Emeryville and bought two round-trip tickets to Sacramento.

We strolled old-town, checked out the railroad museum and had lunch on an old paddle wheeler. On the way home, we passed a farmhouse not far from the tracks. In a very large tree out front was the most wonderful tree-house. She looked at it wistfully and told me how she'd always wanted a tree house, but never got one.

I grabbed the notebook I always carried with me, and much to her delight, we together wrote lyrics that later became my first song for her.

Come Play with Me

Come play with me, we'll build a house up in a tree – a big tree house;
It'll be so high, high up in the sky, and we'll fill it up, just you and I.
Come play with me, we'll build a dream, we'll build a world for you and me;
It'll stretch as far as our hearts can see, and we'll fill it up with possibilities.

> I like playing with you; we both seem to know the rules.
> Will you dance with me underneath the moon?
> Don't be afraid to act the fool.

Come play with me, we'll build a boat, and put to sea where we will float
Between the rolling ocean waves, and the golden light of the Milky Way.

> I like playing with you; we both seem to know the rules.
> Will you dance with me underneath the moon?
> Don't be afraid to act the fool.

Come play with me, we'll build a dream, we'll build a world for you and me.
It'll stretch as far as far as our hearts can see, and we'll fill it up, just you and me.

She laughed with delight as we figured out each verse, but more important to me was that she leaned on my shoulder and wrapped her hands around my arm for the entire trip home. It was a very good day.

Chapter Nineteen: *Before the Beginning*

"My dear husband. I ran into your parents again today. I have to say, they are so cute together. Barbara told me that Pat grew up on an Oklahoma farm and that his favorite pet was a baby pig. She told me you even have a picture of your dad as a small child hugging that pig.

Your dad told me that one day, that pig just disappeared and his folks told him he probably just went wandering away. He suspects it really ended up on the dinner table, but grampa and gramma never copped to it.

Calvin (although everyone called him Pat) regaled me with stories of his childhood. He and his older brother found an old stove pipe. They hid it at the back of the property because the next farm over grew the best watermelons around. On a hot and dusty summer day, he and his brother would grab that stove pipe and sneak into the neighbor's watermelon patch. Pat would hold the melon up on end, and his brother would shove that stovepipe right down the middle. Then they would pull out that center section and enjoy the sweet melon heart with juice running down their chins and onto their shirts. Good summer days.

He told me how they found an old Model A abandoned in a field. They pushed it all the way home and started tinkering with it. That started a lifetime love affair. Pat loved working on cars and tinkering with the engines. They eventually got it running. Of course, neither of them was old enough to get a license, but that didn't bother them at all. They discovered that the wheels of the old car exactly matched the width of the rails of the train tracks that ran past the farm and right through nearby Ada.

So, they drove that car over near the tracks, and took the tires off. Now the rims could run along the tracks. They waited until the morning train passed through, then rolled the car up onto a crossing and guided the wheels onto the tracks. Then they were off to town! They ran the car right down the tracks and into town. They got some candy then ran back up the tracks to get home. They said their parents never had any idea what they'd done, but your grandmother gave me a knowing wink. You can't hide much from a mother.

Just like my own kids. They thought they got away with all sorts of things…. But I knew. I also knew they were responsible enough either not to do anything dangerous (or not get caught doing it). You hear that, boys? I knew.

Keith, your father was a man of the land and never lost his desire to farm. I see where you got your love of gardening, and your sense of adventure and mischief. I always loved that about you. And I see how your father never lost his sense of humor, even while struggling with health issues that took his life far too young. You are very much your father's son, and I love you for it.

Know that your parents and grandparents still love you deeply. They are healthy here and take pride and joy in your life's journey. Know you are connected to them and so many others, not just by blood, but by love...those on earth, and in heaven. I have more to tell you, and I promise to write again soon. Your Marianna."

Chapter Twenty: *Parents*

When I was young, I didn't want to be anything like my father. I thought I was better than he. I was smarter, eventually taller, more successful. I was so damned smug in my "I'm better than my dad" vibe. Boy, was I wrong! In later years, I came to appreciate what I inherited from my parents: humor, steadfastness, determination, empathy, taking care of each other, my love of gardening and music. These are all direct gifts from my parents and they are priceless.

After I graduated from grammar school, I wanted to attend seminary. I felt that I could serve God and my church by becoming a priest. Unbeknownst to me, that school charged monthly tuition, and it was not cheap. My folks never discussed that at all. I'm sure that it was a heavy burden for them, but they never said a word. At the end of my first year, they let me know that I'd have to come home because they could not continue to pay the tuition. I let the rector know that I would not be returning and why. But he said they'd work something out and that I should plan on returning the next year.

It turned out that there was a kind woman in town who owned an apple juice production company in the city where the school was. They told her of my plight, and without hesitation, she offered to pay my tuition for the remaining 3 years! Through the generosity of a total stranger, I was able to continue my education. I still say thankful prayers for this wonderful benefactor. She didn't know me, but did not hesitate to help. There ARE wonderful people in this world.

But parents aren't the only ones who form us. There was Dan. He was a young adult in the employ of a commercial newspaper delivery service… the ones who put newspapers in stacks at the grocery stores and in the vending machines. When I was in sixth grade, I got a job on weekends with this company. I was what they called a "swapper." I would help put the papers together, load them into trucks, then ride along on one of the trucks. The driver would go to the destinations, then the swapper would jump out of the truck and "swap out" the old papers for the new.

At this point, I was a pudgy kid. Much more of a bookworm than an athelete. I was assigned to Dan. The first thing he told me when I joined him was "Kid, you're really fat. I'm going to fix that." He drove me very hard and I hated him for it. He gave me only so much time to swap out the papers, and drove off if I didn't get back in time. I'd have to wait around for him to finish the route before he'd drive back to pick me up. But… over the course of that summer, I slimmed down a lot and learned how to run. I became tougher, doing my job in good weather and bad. I was able to join the school football and basketball teams the following year. He taught me I could work harder and accomplish more than I thought. He was a teacher to me, and I now thank him for the lessons he taught me.

Another parent in my life was my godfather. After my dad passed away, he took over. He'd check on me regularly and let me know that there were people looking out for me. He became a second father to me. And the priests. They were ersatz parents to me while in seminary. They saw to my formation as a young man of faith, made sure I studied hard, and required me to participate in athletic events, and hard farm labor (we grew our own food and raised cattle and other animals). Through those years, I learned compassion and discipline. I learned how to study and pray. Every one of those priests had a hand in forming me… they were my fathers away from home.

And how about myself? There's a saying: "The boy is father to the man." The person I molded myself to be during my teen years, is the person I became as an adult. Discipline, faith, hard work, scholarship, teamwork. The things I did set the framework for the man I would become.

We are parented by many people. Just like there are many flavors of "family," there are also many people who form and parent us along our journey. I am grateful to every one of them.

It is odd to include Marianna here; strange to think of a spouse as a parent (I know, that sounds incestuous but isn't what I mean). She also molded me over the course of our years together. She taught me to open my mind to other views of life. She was a big believer in Rudolf Steiner and Buddhism. It opened my mind to other spiritualities.

Perhaps strangest of all was that she inadvertently taught me how to live in the now. When we met, I was very much a future oriented man. I was always planning the next thing and the one after that. I was so busy mapping out the future, I had lost track of how to enjoy the now.

Her disease changed all that. As Alzheimer's took over her brain, she lost memory and executive functions. She could no longer anticipate or plan. She could not see the future. In her declining mental state, the only thing she knew was "right now." She lived in an eternal now – no memory of the past, and no ability to conceive of the future. As her caregiver, I had to meet her in that place, and over time, her needs molded me into someone with a deep appreciation for the now. I have her and the disease to thank for that great gift.

Chapter Twenty-One: *Gaia*

———⊷∘⚮∘⊶———

"My dear Keith. I know you always thought that my beliefs in Gaia, mother earth, homeopathic medicine, planting and harvesting biodynamically in the moon cycle, and such were a lot of, let me see, how did you put it? Oh yeah... a bunch of hooey. Well, this is a case, my dear husband, where I get to say: "I told you so."

From Heaven, I can so clearly see what is meant by Gaia. The idea that all of earth is connected through a spirit of mother earth that connects all things: rocks and stones, trees and plants, rivers and oceans, and all living beings from the least to the greatest. They -are- all connected after all. I can see all the elements and earth itself glowing with the energy of the Creator. All things working in harmony to sustain and support all the living beings and inanimate structures. Gaia is really another manifestation of God's spirit in the world. All things created work together for the good of all. Just as you and I are still joined by love, so everything on, in and under the earth are connected as well. Made of the same atomic and sub-atomic particles. The atoms that make you up, are the same as the atoms in the stars. Those that make up rocks and air and water, are the same as those that make up humanity and every living thing on earth.

They are all inextricably bound in a co-dependent universe. Even those you do not yet know about, thriving in the waters and crevices deep underground and still inaccessible to science. They will be found one day, but it's just another connection. The native peoples of North America had a deep understanding of this complex web, and they properly saw themselves as caretakers of the earth, not its masters. Look to the middle eastern mystics, and the ancient religious philosophies of India, China and Tibet. They acknowledge this complex web that joins us with all of creation. Gaia is real and is an aspect of God within and around us.

Everywhere there is evidence of life's connections and how we fit into the web of creation. From here, I can see it as glowing energy pulsing throughout the planet and every living thing. You are an integral part of that world. You are part of everyone you meet.

Please take comfort in this. Meditate on that and see that you are in intimate relationship with the whole world and everyone there. I am in you, you are in me, all of humanity and the world is a part of you, and you are part of them all. You are never alone, and you are not without love and care. I see that you are emerging from your depression and that your grief is lessening. I see also that you feel guilty that you are not still grieving as deeply as before.

Please know, my dear, dear Keith, that I applaud your efforts to move on. You will never forget me, nor I, you. I want you to feel happiness again. I want you to smile. I want you to appreciate the great beauty all around you. Rejoin the world and find reasons to get up each day and greet it with love and energy and enthusiasm.

I will write again soon, my love. Your Marianna."

Chapter Twenty-Two: *Gaia Again*

I smiled as I read her letter. We did have many spirited discussions about Gaia and the great mother spirit. I didn't take her biodynamic farming, nor her woo-woo beliefs in a great mother earth seriously. So, I just smiled and said: "You could be right. I guess we'll find out after we die." Well, here we are, aren't we?

I guess I really do have to reconsider my closed-mindedness toward her beliefs in this system. I did really listen to her, and I wrote a song about it from her perspective.

Gaia

Sometimes I am lonely and confused; and the
   fabric of my life's no longer whole.
Deadlines and timelines, I feel used;
   and unkind words of strangers bruise my soul.
I go to the mountains, sit beneath an ancient tree.
   I listen to the murmur of a stream.
I close my eyes and rest in the shadow of the leaves,
   and listen as Gaia speaks to me.

     And she says: "Be at peace, my child.
      Close your eyes, rest in peace."
     And she says: "Be at peace, my child.
      Listen to the wisdom of the trees."

When my soul is crowded, crushed and cowed,
   and the world is pressed so close I can't see;
Lost in the rush and rhythm of the crowd,
   I can't think, I can't feel, I can't breathe.
I go to the ocean and raise a cool white sail;
   I catch the wind and sail upon the sea.
I close my eyes and drift in the kingdom of the whales,
   and listen as Gaia speaks to me.

     And she says: "Be at peace, my child.
      Close your eyes, rest in peace."
     And she says: "Be at peace, my child.
      Listen to the wisdom of the seas."

I was lost and searching all alone
   for things I was unable to define;
Seeking peace and love and a home,
   I was weary of the wanderings of my mind.
You found me on the road, took me in your arms,
   gave me rest and shelter from the storm.
Your kisses revived me, kept me safe and warm,
   whispered words that soothed my aching soul.
      And love says: "Be at peace, my child.
        Close your eyes, rest in peace."
      And love says: "Be at peace, my child.
        Listen to your heart and be free."

Marianna was my Gaia, my north star, my teacher, my partner, my lover. She taught me so very much about what it means to love and open my mind to the beauty and truth all around me. She gave me pause to think and wonder. She made me appreciate the world in a much broader way than if I'd been left to my own devices.

I miss her so very much. I miss the way she challenged me and taught me and loved me without conditions. But what have I to complain about? Here she is, still holding me and healing me from the next life.

I miss you, my Marianna. I love you still, and hold you closely in my mind. I hope your letters go on forever, my dear heart. Forever, until the day I join you where you are.

Chapter Twenty-Three: *One more for the Road*

"My dear Keith. This may be my last letter to you. When I arrived, I knew I had unfinished business with you and I was so blest to be able to send these letters to you, my love. But now I see that you are on your feet and moving toward healing your grief. That was what I yearned for and now you are well on the road to accomplishing that and re-engaging with the world.

In addition, I am more settled here, and deeply engaged with my mission. I have -so- many stories bubbling up out of me, and they speak to those who need to hear them. I was a storyteller on earth and I continue that in Heaven. It is fulfilling and helpful and uplifting here, just as it was on earth.

I am not abandoning you dear husband. I am in you and with you always. If you close your eyes, you can surely feel me in your heart, and sense my hand in yours. Never doubt my love... or God's... or your parents and grandparents. There are a host of those here who love you and lift you up. Know that you are surrounded and filled with the love and faith of those who are eternally in your corner.

Grieve me no longer, but rejoice for my own joy and contentment. Let your love beam into the world and it will be returned to you many-fold. Never lose faith or hope. Smile at each new day. Enjoy the sun and the rain, quiet times, and stormy weather. You are part of it all. Sustain your friends as their love sustains you. Know that I am waiting for you. Your Marianna."

Chapter Twenty-Four: *And Miles to Go…*

I wept freshly as I read her most recent missive. I would not hear from her anymore and that saddened me. But what a gift I was given in her letters. Reassurance and love from beyond. She lifted me up (as her love always did), and gave me joy and hope for tomorrow.

And she is right. I can feel her hand in mine still. I can feel her laying beside me and breathing peacefully next to me at night. I pull back the curtains in the morning, and smile at the new day. I thank God and Marianna for each new day, and the potential joy and beauty it may contain.

This has been my private journey of recovery from deep grief, and I'm glad you have chosen to share it with me. Please know that my unshakeable belief is that we are all still connected with those who have moved on. If you're suffering from a recent loss, know that there is still goodness and love in the world.

Close your eyes and recall those you love. Perhaps you can feel their hand in yours, and their calming, loving presence all around and within you. They are there if you only have faith and love to believe it and see it.

Love each other as we are so deeply loved ourselves. Thank you for taking the time to join me in this brief journey. Signing off, but still holding my dear wife's hand.

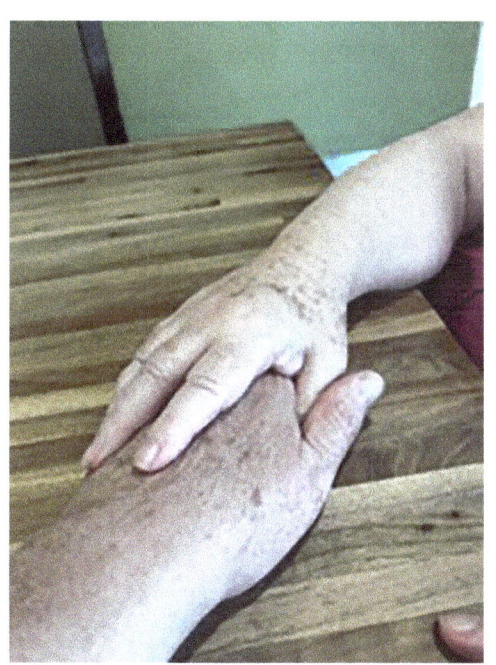

www.ingramcontent.com/pod-product-compliance
Lightning Source LLC
Chambersburg PA
CBHW051549120626

46551CB00013B/1442